BLOODY

MOMENTS

Highlights from the Astonishing History of Medicine
Written by Gael Jennings **+** Illustrated by Roland Harvey

ANNICK PRESS •

TORONTO + NEW YORK + VANCOUVER

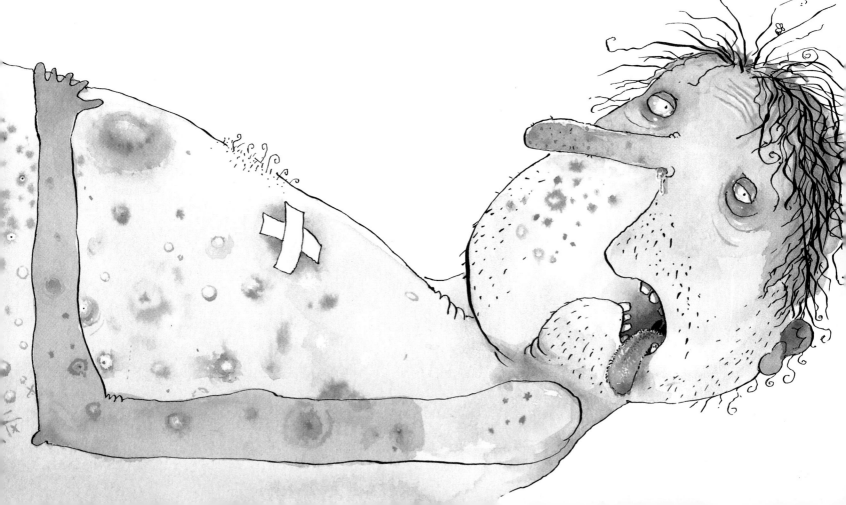

To Anna, Grace and Lola – GJ

To Bug and Gnat – RH

Cataloging in Publication Data

Jennings, Gael
     Bloody moments : (and further highlights from the astonishing history of medicine)

Includes index.
ISBN 1-55037-643-8

1. Medicine – History – Juvenile literature. I. Harvey, Roland. II. Title.

R133.5.J46 2000   j610'.9   C00-930581-5

Distributed in Canada by:
Firefly Books Ltd.
3680 Victoria Park Avenue
Willowdale, ON
M2H 3K1

Published in the U.S.A. by Annick Press (U.S.) Ltd.
Distributed in the U.S.A. by:
Firefly Books (U.S.) Inc.
P.O. Box 1338
Ellicott Station
Buffalo, NY 14205

Film by Eray Scan, Singapore.
Printed by Everbest, China.

visit us at: www.annickpress.com

TABLE OF CONTENTS

He's dodging frantically down the lane, turning to shoot, when BAM, a gun goes off, and his guts explode.

Mabel sighs.

"Bet you two dog biscuits he'll survive," she mutters. Max farts gently in his sleep and doesn't even cock an ear.

Arranged alluringly in some small bandages in the next scene, our muscled hero lounges in his hospital bed, flirting with his glamorous doctor…

SNAP! Mabel eliminates him with the remote control.

She's grumpy. One more shoot-out and miraculous recovery and she'll scream. It's cold and it's wet and all her friends are swanning around somewhere on sunny and exotic holidays while she's dying of a cold, condemned to B-grade re-runs on TV and a geriatric dog. A dog so old he doesn't even remember he has to bark at the letter carrier.

Mabel shuffles to the front door and picks up the slim package that's just plopped through the mail box. And screams.

It's slimy! Flat, square, shiny and wet-feeling; it's an envelope with dark red stains and white glistening bits sticking out of it and it smells sort of sweet. Max snuffles. His nose comes up and he growls but Mabel's heart is pounding now. On the slimy envelope she reads, "The Guts of Human Life".

She drops it. Max's ears are back and his growl is deep in his throat. He totters towards the envelope but Mabel swoops down and grabs the shiny metal disk that has fallen out. It looks like a CD-ROM, but it's deep, glinting red and two-sided.

Mabel peers at one side. "Good Luck", she reads. She flips it over; "Bad Luck". And in tiny script around the middle, "Miracles for Mabel".

Wrrrr click, wwwrrrrr click. The computer screen glows and Mabel stares. It's the same deep red and glowing out of it in sickly yellow are the words: "Good Luck"… and next to it "Bad Luck". With the hair on the back of her neck starting to rise, Mabel's finger moves, all of its own accord, towards the mouse and she clicks on… "Good Luck".

good luck

bad luck

Whooosh... she's pulled, and sucked, and it's dark and it's cold and it's scary, it's a wet field in the middle of the night! There's a heavy mist and all around Mabel can hear men screaming in agony and the muffled sound of cannons and gunshots.

The mist parts and there stands a youngish man in very peculiar clothes, holding a big bag and looking particularly frantic. And well he should. He's knee-deep in blood and guts — a battlefield — with soldiers shattered and gory all around him.

It's 1536, the Siege of Turin, and these poor French soldiers are in the middle of a do-or-die battle with the Italians, and they're dying like flies.

The man with the bag is 26-year-old Ambroise Paré, their surgeon, and BOY! does he have his work cut out for him.

First off, he's not a real surgeon; in 1536, there aren't any. There are only barber-surgeons — they actually start off cutting hair — then they learn to cut flesh. But only diseased and decaying flesh; sort of a cross between butchers and torturers. They do all the revolting things like lancing boils, hacking off arms and legs and sticking leeches on sick people to suck the "bad blood" out.

sucking blood go to page 10 or...

paré's problem go to page 12

The weird practice of "blood-letting" started in prehistoric times, when our hairy ancestors noticed that hippopotamuses who had eaten too much, cut their legs by leaning on sharp reeds, then stopped the bleeding when they felt better by dunking their legs in mud. Most sickness was thought to be due to too much blood, and "bleeding" was all the rage for thousands of years. Some say

American president, George Washington, was bled to death on Friday, December 13, 1799. Blood-letting reached its peak in the 1800s with the French doctor Francoise-Joseph-Victor Broussais, who is rumored to have put fifty leeches at a time on his patients, sucking up, some say, millions of liters of blood in his lifetime!

paré's problem go to page 12

PARE'S PROBLEM

Paré's in a fix. He doesn't know how to delve deep into flesh to fix it and he would kill his patients from shock and pain if he tried, because there aren't any anesthetics. They haven't been invented yet.

Nor can he give the soldiers antibiotics, to kill the germs pouring in through wounds which multiply and cause dreadful fevers, pus-filled ulcers, rotting arms and legs and finally death, because germs won't be discovered for another three hundred years. And the antibiotics which knock them off won't be invented until one hundred years after *that!*

So Paré does what the other state-of-the-art 1536 barber-surgeons do; he pours *boiling oil* into the open wound to stop the bleeding! It's supposed to neutralise the "gunshot poison".

Mabel's stomach churns at the sizzle of burning flesh and a smell reminiscent of Dad's Saturday barbeque.

Paré works bravely on until: DISASTER! At midnight, he runs out of oil! There being no late-night shopping in 1536, Paré rummages around in his bag and makes do – with a mixture of egg yolks, turpentine and oil of roses – which he makes into ointment and rubs on the wounds.

But he can't sleep that night, he's so terrified of what he might discover the next morning. He gets up before dawn and rushes down to the soldiers. And what does he find? The boiling oil group are howling with pain, their wounds red and festering. The ointment group are rested, healing and feeling fine.

Word spreads about this miracle. Ointment takes over from boiling oil. Paré is dubbed the father of modern surgery, and history is changed for ever.

Mabel blinks. "Wow! What GOOD LUCK!"

But you can't do operations with OINTMENT! (Mabel knows from when Max was injured.) You need anesthetics to kill pain, know-how of the body so you cut the right thing, and antibiotics to prevent infections. And as she thinks this, three icons float before her.

Mabel chooses. You choose.

more on paré
go to
page 14

pain
go to
page 16

body
works &
bad ends
go to
page 22

WHAT HAPPENED TO AMBROISE

Wars being all the rage in those days, Ambroise Paré's simple method of healing gunshot wounds saved thousands of soldiers' lives. He went to twenty wars, wrote twenty books and became such a hero that four different French kings hired him as their personal surgeon: Henry II, Francis II, Charles IX and Henry III. He also cured the infertility of Henry II who went on to father ten children, three of whom were kings.

Paré also designed an artificial arm for a French army captain, (remember, this is over 450 years ago!) with catches and springs to let the elbow bend and the fingers open and close, and false legs (which could kneel) and feet. His engineering features for prosthetic limbs are still used today.

Ambroise himself had as many lives as a cat. Even though he was suspected of being the "wrong" religion (a Protestant) and many Catholics tried to poison him, he was protected by Catholic leaders (like the King of France) because they liked his medicine. When he was captured by the enemy on the battlefield, they let him go, because they recognized the man who saved soldiers' lives. He got married at sixty-four, had six kids, the last one when he was seventy-three. He died at eighty.

pain
go to
page 16

body
works &
bad ends
go to
page 22

germs
go to
page 36

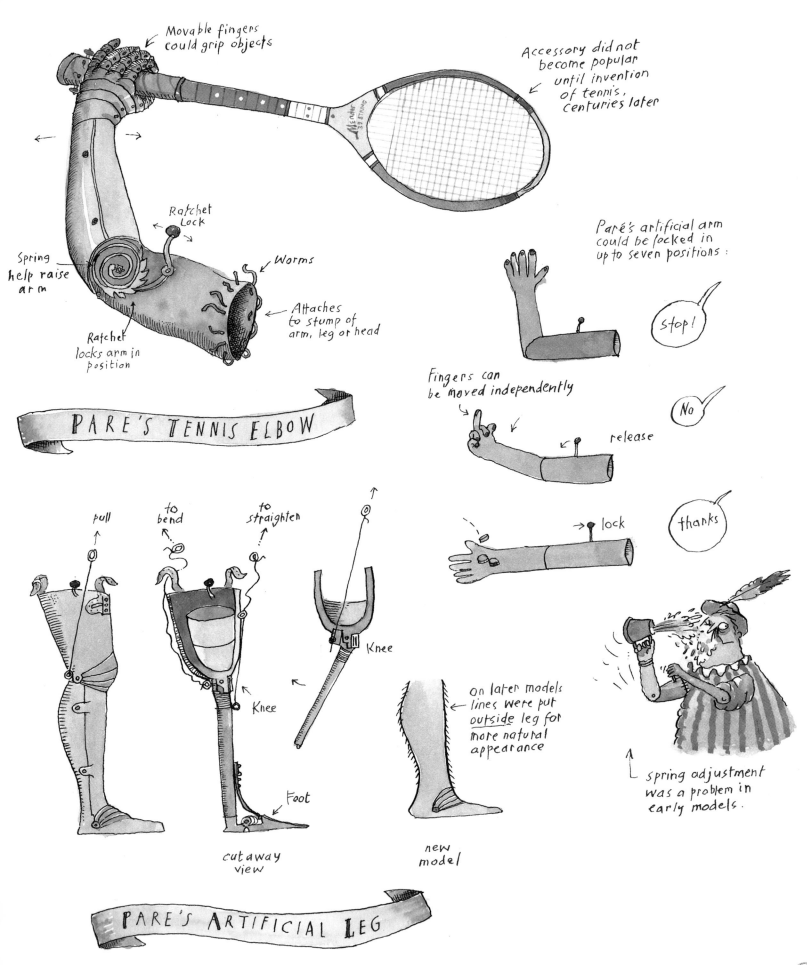

Movable fingers could grip objects

Accessory did not become popular until invention of tennis, centuries later

Ratchet Lock

Spring help raise arm

Worms

Attaches to stump of arm, leg or head

Ratchet locks arm in position

PARE'S TENNIS ELBOW

Paré's artificial arm could be locked in up to seven positions:

stop!

Fingers can be moved independently

No

release

thanks

lock

pull

to bend

to straighten

Knee

Knee

Foot

On later models lines were put outside leg for more natural appearance

cutaway view

new model

spring adjustment was a problem in early models.

PARE'S ARTIFICIAL LEG

PAIN

Mabel is grabbed and flung backwards faster than a rocket, the air whizzing in her ears and then…

On the screen is a filthy hairy woman in a sort of fur sarong. The woman lifts a rock on a stick and WHACK! clubs a man on the head with it! This is prehistoric surgery; cracking the skull to let the demons (headache) out.

Mabel feels a little sick, then – zzzooomph – she's flung forwards and "Slit!" The dagger flashes, the flesh parts, the globby yellow fat oozes with blood, and a baby is pulled from its mother's stomach.

("Oh yuck," says Mabel.) It's baby Julius Caesar – the first Roman Emperor – and the first Caesarean, 81 BC.

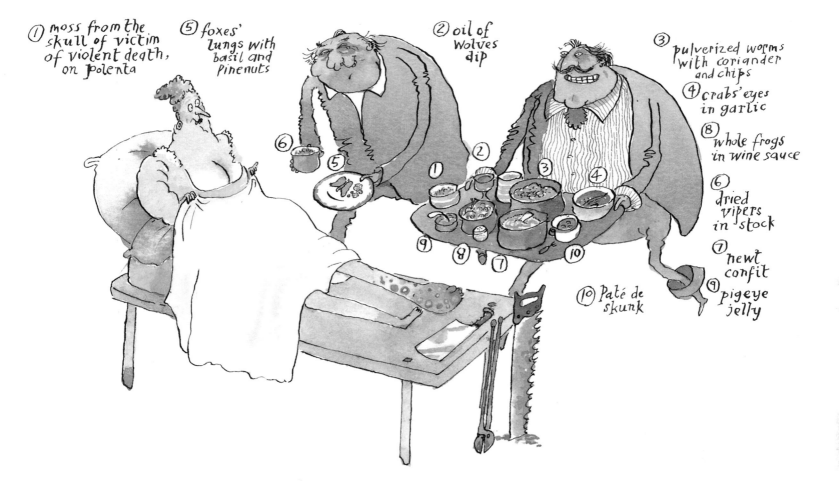

① moss from the skull of victim of violent death, on polenta

⑤ foxes' lungs with basil and pinenuts

② oil of wolves dip

③ pulverized worms with coriander and chips

④ crabs' eyes in garlic

⑧ whole frogs in wine sauce

⑥ dried vipers in stock

⑦ newt confit

⑨ pigeye jelly

⑩ Paté de skunk

Mabel moves on through time. Tonsils are ripped from throats, rotted legs sawn roughly through with blood-caked saws... Mabel is getting the idea as she's zapped from country to country through thousands of years. "Surgery" really hurts! Nothing can put people out cold like today, so they feel every cut. They are offered powdered metals and jewels, revolting bits of animal and a whole range of very weird looking plants, and alcohol, to dull the pain, but nothing puts them to sleep.

As far as Mabel can see, the only thing doctors can do is cut fast. (The world record being Robert Liston in the 1840s, who could amputate a leg in two and a half minutes.) But so fast that lots of mistakes are made. The British quack eye doctor, John "Chevalier" Taylor, superstar of royalty, whisked the hardened lenses out of cataract-ridden eyes so rapidly that he is reliably rumored to have helped make Bach and Handel blind!

Things are looking very grim to Mabel until...

PLOP! Mabel feels like she's been dropped down hard on a wooden bench. It's a hall, crowded, noisy and hot and abuzz with excitement. Men are craning their necks to see the stage.

Under a banner which reads, "Exhilarating and Laughing Gas, Connecticut, December 10, 1844", are twelve young men weeping with laughter, hanging off each other as they take turns in breathing from what looks suspiciously like a red whoopee cushion.

In the audience 29-year-old Horace Wells is not laughing. He's a dentist who can't cure his own throbbing wisdom tooth. He won't even let his partner, Bill, touch it so they've come out to get distracted. A failed doctor called Gardner Colton has put on this show of the "new champagne"; the gas that's tickled the fancy of Samuel Taylor Coleridge and Roget of Thesaurus fame. Nitrous oxide turns even the most crashing bore into the life of the party. Invented seventy-two years before by a young man called Priestley (who also thought up soda water), this laughing gas is certainly hitting the funny bone of the twelve volunteers on the stage.

Suddenly one of them runs amuck, off the stage, crashing through the benches, cutting his knees to ribbons. And he doesn't stop laughing – never feeling a thing!

Horace stares, open-mouthed, then, PING! a light bulb goes off in his head.

He borrows some nitrous oxide from Colton, and the next day, in his own dental chair, Horace breathes the gas in and has his tooth pulled out, completely without pain. Anesthesia is born!

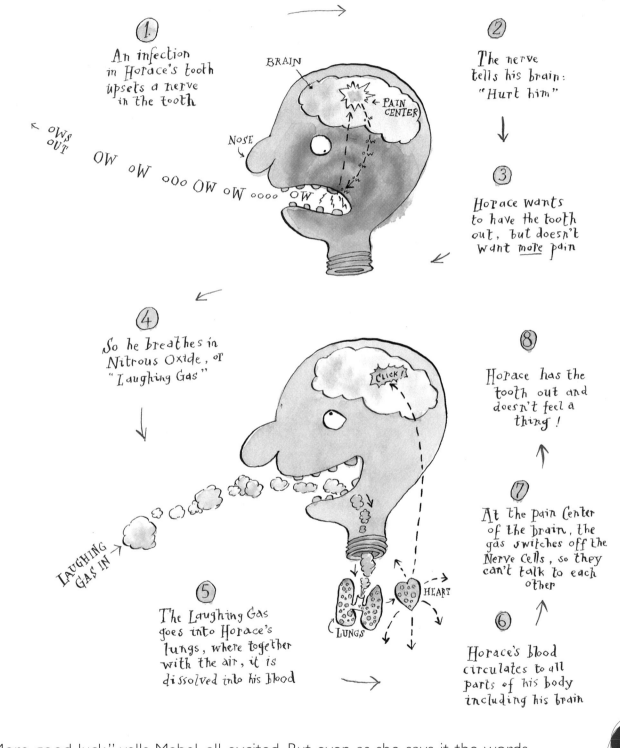

1. An infection in Horace's tooth upsets a nerve in the tooth

BRAIN

PAIN CENTER

NOSE

← OWS OUT OW OW ooo OW oW oooo OW

2. The nerve tells his brain: "Hurt him"

3. Horace wants to have the tooth out, but doesn't want more pain

4. So he breathes in Nitrous Oxide, or "Laughing Gas"

LAUGHING GAS IN →

CLICK!

8. Horace has the tooth out and doesn't feel a thing!

7. At the pain Center of the brain, the gas switches off the Nerve Cells, so they can't talk to each other

HEART

LUNGS

5. The Laughing Gas goes into Horace's lungs, where together with the air, it is dissolved into his blood

6. Horace's blood circulates to all parts of his body including his brain

"More good luck," yells Mabel, all excited. But even as she says it the words

"Bad Luck" swim before her eyes, and her hand reaches forward to touch the mouse…

bad luck go to page 20

BAD LUCK

Horace is dead keen to become a star, so his mate Bill arranges for him to show off his wonderful laughing gas anesthesia to Harvard medical students at the Massachusetts General Hospital. If teeth can be extracted without pain, (it being a 2-person-block-and-tackle-blood-and-guts sort of operation), surely all sorts of other operations could be painless, too?

But Horace bungles it. In front of the Harvard heavies, his anesthetized patient squawks when the tooth is yanked, and Horace is laughed from the room. He gets depressed, leaves town, accidentally kills a patient, gives up dentistry and takes to sniffing far too much of his laughing gas and other silly gases like chloroform and ether. Four short years later, he is arrested for throwing acid over two young women and, high on chloroform, he commits suicide in jail.

Bill though, is another matter. He (William Thomas Green Morton) isn't going to sink without a trace. He swipes Horace's idea, but thinks the gas ether might do better than nitrous oxide (ether having been discovered three hundred years earlier). Bill goes to his ex-landlord, the doctor and chemist, Charles Jackson, for advice on the chemistry of ether.

Bill takes the advice, renames ether "letheon gas" and secretly tries it out as an anesthetic on his dog, a guinea pig, and finally himself.

On September 30, 1846, he

soaks his hanky in it,

looks at his

watch, takes

a deep breath and…

wakes up eight minutes later, feeling just fine! That very night he tries it on one of his dentistry patients and it works wonderfully.

So, Bill too goes off to show the Harvard medical students a thing or two, and his ether anesthetic is a hit. His patient doesn't stir, even when a tumor is removed from his jaw, and the Harvard heavies swoon. Bill is on his way to fame and fortune, but he has overlooked the wily Doctor Jackson!

Jackson is extremely miffed that Bill's going to be rich and famous and he isn't, so Jackson writes to all the important doctors saying he discovered ether. Since he also claims to have invented the electric telegraph before Morse in 1836 (and he probably did) and because Jackson is a doctor and Bill a mere dentist, they believe Jackson.

A twelve-year legal fight over the rights to ether anesthetic starts, and it ends in tragedy in July 1868, when Bill goes to see his lawyer in New York and gets so upset he has a cerebral hemorrhage and dies.

But Bill has the last laugh! It is put on his headstone that he is the "Inventor of Anesthetic Inhalation" and it's said that some years later when Jackson visits the grave, drunk, and reads the inscription, he gets so upset that he goes crazy, and in 1873 he dies, insane, in a mental asylum.

Mabel shakes her head sadly.

Such bad luck, such trouble... oh, no, it's happening again!

The icon appears...

body works & bad ends go to page 22

and she can't resist. Can you?

BODY WORKS

"Catalog of Bad Ends", Mabel reads, and starts to scroll through hundreds of years of human nightmares: beheadings, human bonfires, torture, murder and madness.

It's all very confusing. Mabel scrolls all the way back through 5,000 years then moves slowly forward and begins to get the hang of it.

It seems that just about everywhere, at just about every time until the last few hundred years, people believed that human life and health were connected directly to the cosmos: to planets, water, earth, gods and demons. Medicine wasn't, as it is today, based on scientific understanding of the human body. Curing people and keeping them healthy was about keeping balance with the cosmos and making sure the gods were happy, the demons vanquished, and the soul (rather than the body) in good hands. So medicine was about magic too, and the "doctors" through all that history stayed on the side of the gods. Questioning the gods and the wisdom of the ancients was bad, bad, bad! So dissection of human bodies wasn't done, not in China, India, the Pharaoh's Egypt, Greece or Rome, until…

A few hundred years ago, certain scientists and doctors just had to know what was going on. They started delving into human bodies. They saw all these marvellous things (things quite specifically contradicted by the ancients) bones, muscles, nerves, blood vessels. And, because they believed in what they saw rather than what they were told, they turned on the "cosmos believers" and told them they were wrong. And BOY!... did they pay for the heresy!

There were a lot of bad ends.

Like this poor guy. Mabel stops scrolling.

"Good grief! He's being burnt alive at the stake!"

It's Geneva in 1553; good old Ambroise Paré in next-door France is just teaching people to tie off leg stumps after they have been amputated. But this human sausage sizzle is Spanish; Michael Servetus. His crime has been to use his research on human bodies to criticize just about every type of Christianity going in 1553 (a brave but dangerous move).

Now the Incredibly Upright religious leader, John Calvin, has taken Michael's suggestion that blood circulates around the body and through the lungs, instead of swishing back and forth across the heart like tides (the prevailing belief) as an insult against the Holy Trinity – so – WHOOSH – there Servetus goes, up in flames, fuelled by his own scientific writings.

And here is another bonfire, this time of books, in Padua, Italy, just a few years earlier in 1542. Andreas Vesalius is burning his own magnificent, accurate drawings of the insides of human bodies, including the blood-going-round-the-body diagrams. He's gotten away with stealing the odd corpse hanging from a hook around town (hook-hanging being another popular punishment of the day), sneaking it home to rip off the skin and see all the gorgeous gory bits inside. But when he draws what he sees – the Church turns on him – because he proves, among other things, that Eve couldn't have come from Adam's rib, men and women having the same number. So he torches the evidence and goes to Rome, then Spain, where he specializes in Diseases of the Very Rich, serving the Holy Roman Emperor Charles IV, and Spain's Phillip II.

One day he's up to his arms in blood, dissecting a supposedly dead Spanish nobleman, *when the guy moves* and Vesalius is sentenced to death by the Spanish Inquisition for grave-robbing.

Fed up, he sets off for the Holy Land, and is shipwrecked on an island. He dies, alone and starving, at forty-nine.

His seven great books of intricate drawings of the human body — the blood vessels, guts, muscles, nerves and bones — published in 1543 when Vesalius was just twenty-nine, are confirmed and extended by the Brit, William Harvey, in 1628. Mabel is not so surprised — the Chinese Emperor Huang Ti said that blood circulated 4,500 years before — and Pythagoras in Italy had a pretty fair idea of the body in 500 BC.

Today, Mabel knows, Andreas Vesalius is called the Father of Anatomy. He was the great turning point from cosmic to scientific medicine and his seven volumes of human atlases are the foundation of modern medicine.

Mabel's had enough. She's tired and hungry and her cold is getting worse. How do all these people ever expect to learn anything if they keep killing off or humiliating all of their bright lights? Didn't anyone ever just invent something people wanted?

good luck
go to
page 28

The music starts…

All the blood of the Human Body is under the control of the HEART and is regulated by it. The blood current flows continuously in a circle and never stops.

HUANG TI
CHINA 2698 - 2598 B.C

My Medical School at Croton produced some of the greatest medical scientists in history, some of whom discovered the optic nerve ◉, Eustachian tube §, the difference between veins and arteries, and suggested that the brain was the center of the intellect and senses.

TREVOR PYTHAGORAS OF GREECE
in ITALY 500 B.C

I spent five years carefully observing and experimenting on the human body. Then I wrote seven books on its structure and systems. Then I BURNT them.

ANDREAS VESALIUS
of BRUSSELS 1543

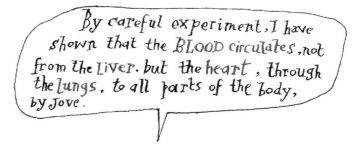

By careful experiment, I have shown that the BLOOD circulates, not from the LIVER. but the heart, through the lungs, to all parts of the body, by Jove.

WILLIAM HARVEY
ENGLAND 1628

GOOD LUCK

Mabel hears an accordion play, the sound of horse-drawn carriages, the whoosh of rustling skirts, and she's in Paris in 1816, watching a **very large** young woman (we're talking big breasts here) waddle into the rooms of Dr René Theophile-Hyacinthe **Laennec**, chest specialist, complaining of heart pains.

Now, the usual way for doctors to check out hearts and lungs, (invented by the Egyptians over 3,000 years ago) is to pop their heads on the patient's chest and listen for **whooshings** and **beatings**.

But this patient presents a big problem (actually, two) for Dr Laennec; he can't get to it!

In the mutually embarrassed silence, he scratches his head and thinks, then grins! Just this morning he saw two children playing in the courtyard of the Louvre; the boy scratching at the end of a wooden pole with a pin, the girl with her ear to the other end of the pole, clearly hearing the scratches and counting them.

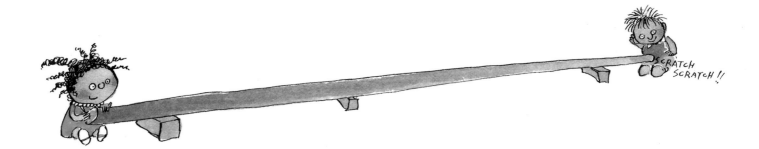

Bingo! Sound travels, and better through solids than air. Laennec immediately snatches up a sheaf of paper, rolls it into a cylinder, ties it with string, and hears the patient's diseased heart more clearly than he has ever heard one beat before.

As soon as she is gone, Dr Laennec (being an amateur cabinet maker) experiments with cylinders of glass, paper, wood and metal, and comes up with… the stethoscope!

He writes a book, becomes incredibly famous, marries his housekeeper, and the stethoscope becomes one of the most important diagnostic tools of medicine, even today.

"Yes!" Mabel punches the air.

MORE ON LAENNEC

It isn't all victory for René Laennec. He dies just ten years later from, ironically, a chest disease, pulmonary TB, the same disease that carries off most of his gunk-filled patients.

Today, he would give these TB patients a chest X-ray, examine their hawked spit for germs, and prescribe anti-TB drugs. But Roentgen didn't discover X-rays until 1895 (he got the first Nobel prize in 1901). The TB bacterium wasn't found by Robert Koch until 1882 (Nobel prize in 1905); and it was only in the 1940s that Selman Waksman created the first successful anti-TB drug; (Nobel prize 1952).

But the stethoscope still stands.

1826 — Poor René dies... of T.B.

Might just watch a little T.B. tonight...

T.B or not T.B.... that is the question.

1882 — Robert Koch discovers tubercle bacillus, the organism which causes T.B....

Roentgen stumbles across X-Ray device while trying to invent submarine

1895 — Roentgen discovers X-Ray... which detects T.B in patients' lungs

* Note: Not to be confused with Selwyn Walkman, who invented the earplug.

1944 — Dr. Selman Waksman* discovers anti-T.B drug.

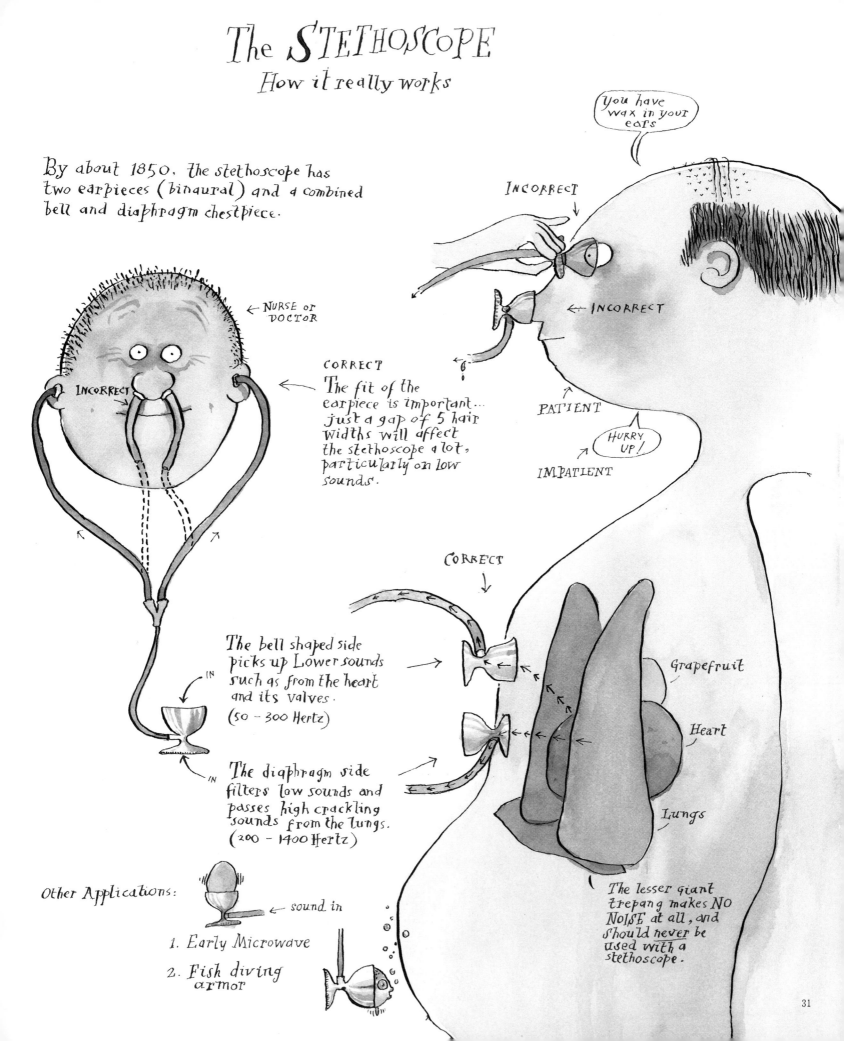

TUMMY TROUBLES

"What on earth are you doing?"

Mabel whips around, sees her mother at the door, and spread-eagles the screen, desperate to keep her miracle a secret. But her mother is so relieved that Mabel is away from the wretched TV that she banishes the suspicion that there is some nasty chat room on there, and calls "Dinner's ready" as she wafts from the room. Mabel's tummy rumbles. Behind her the screen does too… Mabel can't resist… just one more look.

It's a peep-hole into… a stomach. This is not a good look. Attached to the stomach is the rest of Alexis St Martin. He's not pleased to be a human-show-and-tell, but he is relieved he's not dead. Not many people in 1822 survive gunshots blasting out their guts.

Al had been trapping animals in the wilds of Canada, and had returned to an island in the middle of nowhere (a lake between Canada and the USA to be precise), sold his animal pelts and had a few drinks to celebrate, when BAM, one of his drunken mates tripped over his gun and the rest was history.

Alexis had thought he was lucky that the American doctor, William Beaumont, was there to save his life, but when Al's wound healed into a perfect 15 cm hole (6 inch) straight into his stomach, Beaumont took this golden opportunity to discover first-hand how stomachs work.

Canny Beaumont gets Alexis to sign a contract saying he's willing to be used as a human guinea pig. He gets Al to eat different things, then sees what happens inside. He makes Al swallow meat on a string and then pulls it out again and examines it. He measures the goo from Al's stomach, before, during, and after different meals (there's more goo during) and syphons it off to test it. Al is horrified to find out it is partly hydrochloric acid.

For eleven long years, Al puts up with Beaumont's experiments. Beaumont gets rich and famous for discovering the secrets of digestion. Al just gets angry.

The screen shifts.

Slimy yellow lumps, globs of green and brown.

Mabel's looking at the vomit of Lazzaro Spallanzani two hundred years ago, and so is Lazzaro! He keeps eating his own vomit and throwing it up again to see how it changes. It just gets runnier and runnier.

Mabel feels sick.

And here's a French guy, Claude Bernard, a hundred years later, kidnapping dogs and draining the juice from their guts to see what it does to lumps of fat. (It makes them disintegrate.)

The miracles of digestion are slowly uncovered.

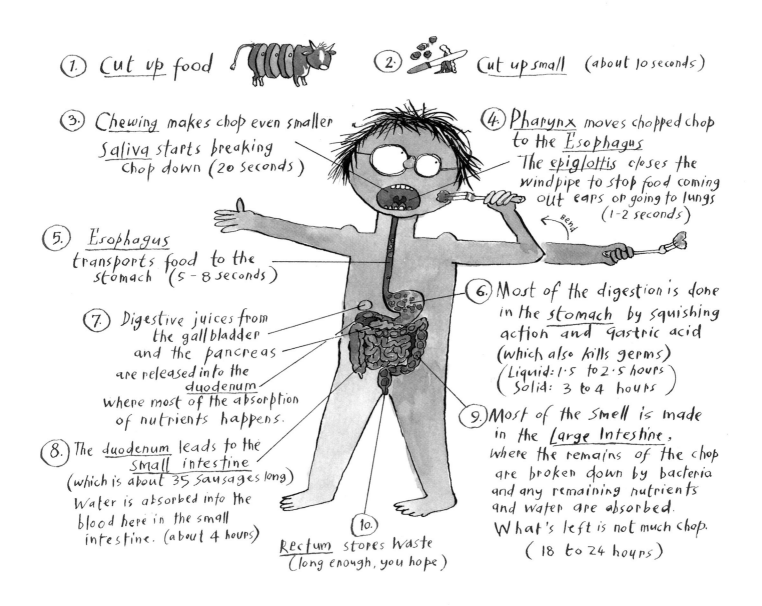

1. Cut up food

2. Cut up small (about 10 seconds)

3. Chewing makes chop even smaller. Saliva starts breaking chop down (20 seconds)

4. Pharynx moves chopped chop to the Esophagus. The epiglottis closes the windpipe to stop food coming out ears or going to lungs (1-2 seconds)

5. Esophagus transports food to the stomach (5-8 seconds)

6. Most of the digestion is done in the stomach by squishing action and gastric acid (which also kills germs) (Liquid: 1.5 to 2.5 hours) (Solid: 3 to 4 hours)

7. Digestive juices from the gall bladder and the pancreas are released into the duodenum where most of the absorption of nutrients happens.

8. The duodenum leads to the small intestine (which is about 35 sausages long). Water is absorbed into the blood here in the small intestine. (about 4 hours)

9. Most of the smell is made in the Large Intestine, where the remains of the chop are broken down by bacteria and any remaining nutrients and water are absorbed. What's left is not much chop. (18 to 24 hours)

10. Rectum stores waste (long enough, you hope)

THE LIFE STORY OF MABEL'S LAMB CHOP
by Ali Mentary

"Mabel… dinner!" Good timing, Mom.

The screen fades to an inky black and the shiny wet disk ejects itself. Mabel slips it behind the fish tank and hurries to the table to try a little digestion of her own.

Later, wondering queasily what state her lamb chops are now in, Mabel sits before the screen again, waiting for the familiar wrrring and clicking. She idly picks her teeth as the disk takes hold and…

germs die

go to page 36

This is really weird…

GERMS DIE

The screen's full of short wriggly worms darting around, forming chains, and vibrating. But then they zoom away, getting smaller and smaller, until…

Mabel's looking at a man who, in turn, is looking down at the "worms" through a tiny microscope.

It's Holland, September 17, 1683, and the man is 51-year-old Dutch draper Antony van Leeuwenhoek. Tony's not an educated man (although the great painter Vermeer was his best buddy before he died fifteen

years earlier), but he does love cutting glass, and he's fashioned a simple microscope under which he zaps everything he can lay his hands on: bees, weeds, algae.

sperm

bogeys (snot)

In fact, Tony's the first person in the world to see sperm, red blood cells, the compound eyes of insects, and one-celled plants. Tsar Peter of Russia and hundreds of others will flock to see these miracles. But today, Tony's just had dinner and he's picked his teeth and put what he found under the microscope. What he sees amazes him.

I don't know what it is, but boy, it's ugly

"I then most always saw, with great wonder, that… in the said matter, there were many very little living animalcules, very prettily are a-moving… in such enormous numbers that all the water… seemed to be alive."[1]

He's looking at living germs; live bacteria. The first person ever to see them.

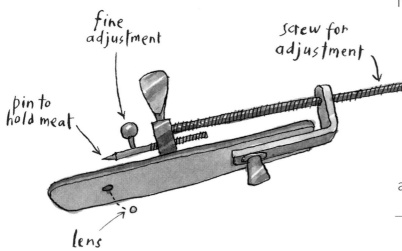
fine adjustment
screw for adjustment
pin to hold meat
lens

Now, this is a mind-blowing breakthrough, only Tony doesn't know it… It's the first step towards saving hundreds of millions of lives from fatal infections. Because if there are "living germs" swarming everywhere, they can spread, invade bodies, multiply and, if they're bad germs – kill.

you want to know how bad? go to page 40

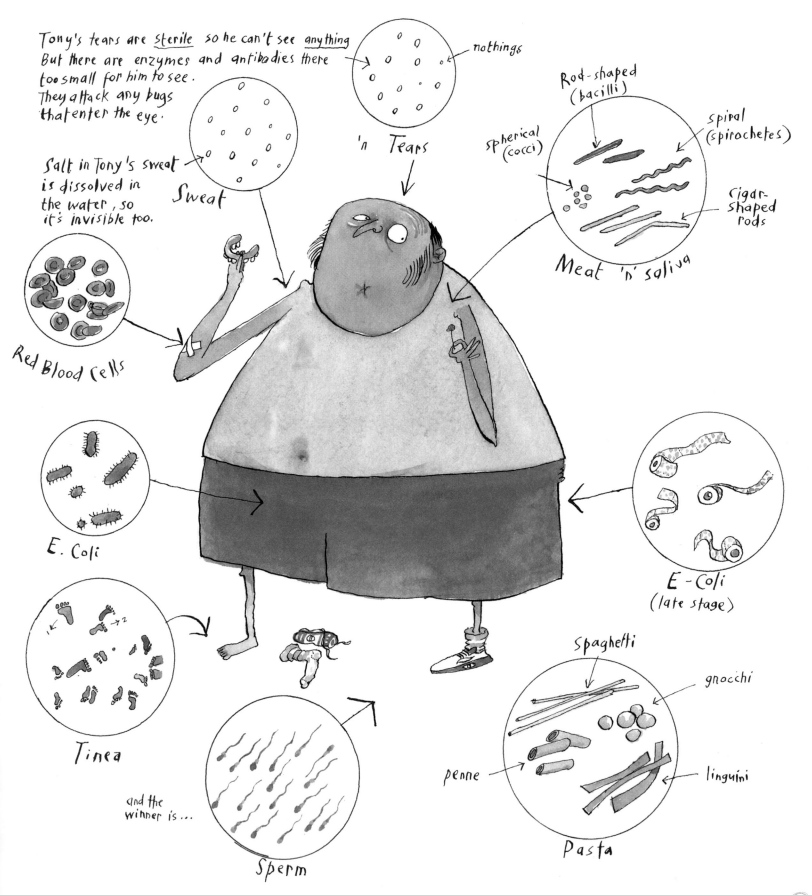

Tony's tears are <u>sterile</u> so he can't see <u>anything</u>. But there are enzymes and antibodies there too small for him to see. They attack any bugs that enter the eye.

nothings

'n Tears

Salt in Tony's sweat is dissolved in the water, so it's invisible too.

Sweat

Rod-shaped (bacilli)

spherical (cocci)

spiral (spirochetes)

cigar-shaped rods

Meat 'n' saliva

Red Blood Cells

E. Coli

E-Coli (late stage)

Tinea

and the winner is...

Sperm

Spaghetti

gnocchi

penne

linguini

Pasta

It explains all the plagues and epidemics, where something was clearly spreading death, and all the lives lost from infected wounds in battle, on operating tables, and after accidents.

But, right now, in Tony's time, no one has a clue about germs. They all think infections are caused by angry gods, bad air, or invisible poisonous particles.

And because Tony's only seen live germs, not proven they cause infections, people go on believing it is only bad air… for nearly 200 years, until…

fight back!
germs go down!
strike 1
go to
page 42

Shady dark corridors…

YOU WANT TO KNOW HOW BAD?

Rotting black legs, weeping yellow sores, mouths paralyzed in agonized screams; bad germs kill badly. And there are thousands of deadly types; either catchy ones which cause epidemics, or wound ones which creep in through rips in the skin.

The catchy ones are the most important and are bacteria, which can mostly be killed by antibiotics, viruses (which can't) or parasites. The nastiest catchy ones are probably:

The Black Plague
— wiped out tens of millions of people between 100 BC and 1994, from Asia to Europe, killing a quarter of Europe (20 million people) in the 4 years between 1346 and 1350 alone. A rodent disease, a single bite of an infected flea from a rat injects 24,000 Yersinia bacteria into a person. Two-thirds of those people bitten, die.

Smallpox
— first documented as killing an Egyptian Pharaoh in 1160 BC, then 5 million people in 2nd century Europe. Moving in waves of infection, it caused one-tenth of all deaths in the 17th century and had claimed 60 million lives by the 18th century. It is caused by the poxvirus and spread in droplets from the nose and mouth, but was successfully wiped from the face of the earth in November 1974 after a global vaccination program.

Influenza
— the most mobile and lethal pandemics the world has ever seen. The flu virus killed 25 million people in the six months after the end of World War 1 in 1918 (three times as many dead as in that war). It is a virus spread in air from nose and mouth. Still no cure.

HIV/AIDS
— about 42 million people now infected, 90 % of them in developing countries, and nearly 12 million dead. The HIV virus is spread by contact of blood or sexual fluids with those of an infected person. Still no cure.

back to page 39

THOMAS SMITH ... WORLD'S SICKEST MAN · 1352 A.D.

Poor Thomas has four basic types of disease : PARASITIC, FUNGAL, BACTERIAL & VIRAL

God, I feel awful

Ringworm →

One of Thomas' more attractive ailments is SMALLPOX, a VIRUS. He has a rash, a fever and will die from it.

T.B. bacteria (tuberculosis) is carried by water droplets affect Thomas' lungs and other organs.

PLAGUE bacteria give Tom sweats, black tongue, black spots, inflamed boils in the groin and armpits before he DIES. The bacteria can live for a long time in spit, dead bodies and soil ... WAITING ...

SYPHILIS: Like Henry VIII, Tom could die from it, a spirochete bacteria passed by sexual contact and VERY CATCHY. It's a pity antibiotics haven't been invented yet.

CHOLERA is a bacterial infection of the small intestine, from   in the WATER or FOOD. Cholera kills half of its victims ... don't know which half.

GONORRHEA is a bacterial infection which can be VERY HARD TO SPELL. It is spread by sexual contact with an infected person and is really really DISGUSTING.

TETANUS bacteria have invaded Tom's CENTRAL NERVOUS SYSTEM. They are some of the most DEADLY POISONS KNOWN. Tetanus causes headache, lockjaw and violent spasms in every muscle in his body.

The FLU virus is affecting Tom's RESPIRATORY and INTESTINAL SYSTEMS.

← Smallpox

Thomas didn't have a watch. If he had one it would have stopped.

Plague boils

← Plague spots

Typhoid

Ringworm ↓

Plague boils →

← Cholera

Tom's right knee was in beautiful condition except for the arthritis.

Shortly after Tom was bitten by a RABID corgi, his LEPROUS leg fell off at the knee.

Dysentery →

The MALARIA parasite is carried by mosquitoes from other infected people or a CESSPOOL where they breed. Poor Tom gets fever, chills, enlarged spleen, and VERY SICK.

Thomas also has TYPHOID, a bacterial infection by SALMONELLA TYPHI, from contaminated food or water. Not that he'll really notice, but he has fever, rashes, and diarrhea, not to mention bleeding and lovely rosy spots.

On his way to visit his mother, Tom got bitten by a SKUNK. Unfortunately it had RABIES, a deadly VIRUS which goes along nerve paths to the BRAIN and then other organs.

DYSENTERY: Thomas' INTESTINE is inflamed, possibly by any (or all) of: , BACTERIA, PROTOZOA and PARASITES. Poor Tom has bad pain, bloody feces and spasms. SOMEONE didn't WASH their HANDS!

LEPROSY bacteria destroy many systems in THOMAS' body, including Tissue, Bone, Cartilage and Nerves. Eyesight, voice, fingers, feet and hands rot away over 15 to 20 years and you can't even scratch your ...

... TINEA, a fungus, also called Athlete's Foot. If Thomas had sneakers they would SMELL. If Tom's mom had told him to dry his feet properly, he might have had more girlfriends.

P.S. He also has JOCK ITCH and RINGWORM

Tom needed to be very tall to fit all the diseases in. He died after being run over by a cart while coming home from gym.

FIGHT BACK!
GERMS GO DOWN!
STRIKE 1

Ignaz is on the hunt for a killer. He's a 29-year-old Hungarian child birth doctor (obstetrician) and he can't work out why the women in one ward of his Vienna hospital are all dying from **high fevers** after having their babies, yet the new mothers in another ward aren't.

It's 1847, and everyone says it's because of "bad air", but the air's the same in the two wards. The only difference Iggy can see (Ignaz Philippe Semmelweiss) is that the women who die are examined by medical students, arms still caked in blood and pus from the autopsies they have just done; while the healthy women are tended by midwifery trainees (who don't do autopsies).

Then Iggy's friend, Dr Kolletschka, dies from the same sort of fever as the women after cutting himself with a scalpel during an autopsy.

42

Iggy nails the culprit. There's something living and deadly being passed from the gore of the dead bodies, to the doctor's hands and into the wombs of the new mothers as they are examined!

He has to kill it – so he invents – hand washing! (Soap had already been created from goat fat and caustic wood ash by the Phoenicians in 600 BC, when they noticed people stayed healthier when clean, but the practice was lost as cities grew more crowded.)

Iggy introduces chlorinated water for washing, the doctors scrub up, and the death rate nosedives!

But what's this? Mabel can't believe it! – the "Establishment" doctors sneer at Ignaz – they still like the bad air theory. They stop the hand washing, and the death rate soars again.

Iggy, despairing, retires to his native Budapest, and eighteen years later cuts his finger while doing an autopsy. Germs swarm from the bloody body up into his blood, to fester in his finger, his lungs and his brain, and he goes mad with the same fever from which he saved so many women. He dies in an asylum just forty-seven years old.

But wait…

just one year after that…

STRIKE 2
AUGUST 12, 1865, SCOTLAND

A boy about Mabel's age called Jimmy Greenlees is screaming, his broken bone jutting out from his leg. Leaning over him, Dr Joseph Lister is conducting an experiment.

Lister, like Iggy eighteen years before him, reckons invisible living things get into wounds to make people sick and die. The same sorts of living specks that sometimes make the wine his father sells go off.

So he'd looked around for something that would kill those living invaders, and settled on carbolic acid (already used to clean up sewage) diluted with linseed oil and soaked onto lint, and right now, he's dabbing it on Jimmy's leg.

Six weeks later, Jimmy's healthy as an ox.

Lister starts his assault on the germs of surgery.

He bottles the carbolic acid, and sprays it (like a perfume) all over the operating

theaters at the Glasgow hospital where he is professor of surgery. In his day they looked like slaughter

houses – blood splattered on walls, gore clotting in sand on the floor, basins of pus and guts,

and doctors still caked in blood. He puts the acid in a steam engine and puffs it over patient, doctor

and nurse alike, and instead of one in two patients dying, only one in every seven does.

The Prussians take his engine to the Franco-Prussian war of

1870 and save hundreds of wounded

soldiers' lives, and Queen Victoria herself allows

him to spray her royal armpit before cutting

out a festering abscess.

one for
the women
strike 3
go to
page 46

The battle against bugs proceeds.

ONE FOR THE WOMEN
STRIKE 3

A woman with a lamp rustling in the dark along rows of soldiers gored in battle.

It's Turkey, 1854, and 34-year-old Florence Nightingale has defied society and her parents (nice girls get married and stay home) to nurse the dying British soldiers at the Crimean War.

Florence sneers at the "bad air" theory. The men are drinking water that's contaminated with their feces, the food is teeming with maggots and weevils, the wounds are slimy with pus. It is obvious to her that "dirtiness" is what's killing the soldiers, and she acts.

Hands, wounds, clothes and surgical instruments are washed. Water is purified. Soon, instead of sixty out of every one hundred men dying, only two do.

Florence returns home to England a hero, and ignores it. She sets up a proper school for nurses; a good thing, since nurses in London in 1860 were described by writers like Charles Dickens as loud-mouthed, tipsy, ignorant slouches. In fact, conditions in hospitals were so appallingly dirty that only the desperate would work there. And, while Joe Lister is spraying his carbolic acid around surgeries, Florence Nightingale gathers facts. Patients surviving in dirty hospitals versus patients surviving in clean hospitals.

Clean hospitals win hands down, and Florence is finally able to force those in charge to introduce cleanliness. Wards, instruments, floors, patients, doctors, nurses are all scrubbed. Going to hospital is no longer a death sentence.

strike 4
go to
page 48

STRIKE 4

Mabel is triumphant. They're on the trail now!

It's the US in the late 1880s and surgeons are now scrubbing their hands. But at John Hopkins Hospital, Dr William Halstead is very worried about his head surgical nurse, Miss Caroline Hampton. She scrubs so hard her hands are red-raw. William goes off to the Goodyear Rubber Company and comes back with the first pair of surgical rubber gloves! Miss Hampton marries him, and even food handlers have to wear gloves today.

But something doesn't feel right to Mabel. Medicine seems to be going ahead at a good pace, but Florence Nightingale (and the gloved Miss Hampton) are the only women who seem to have done anything. Mabel knows women are great doctors; her mother is one, and in her Aunt Grace's medical course, half the class is female. So where are all the women heroes in Mabel's medical miracles?

The computer hisses at her and shakes, and the screen bursts into flames.

bad luck
go to
page 49

BAD LUCK

Terrible flames, howling women, burning flesh. Germany in 1555, America in 1692. Women who deal in potions and herbs to help the sick are being burnt at the stake as witches. Stomach churning, Mabel zooms in close to get a clearer picture, and sees that these women aren't witches, they are healers. Men are so spooked by their seemingly magical powers that they burn them.

In fact, Mabel peers and peers as she scrolls through thousands of years, and hundreds of countries… there's nothing unusual in this women and healing business. It wasn't just in the "witch" times. Women, it appears, have always been just as important as men in medicine, just in a completely different way.

Throughout history women have been the background health-givers; in charge of the entire community's health. They knew what foods were good and provided them. They nursed the sick, the old and the poor. They delivered babies and folk remedies. They performed minor surgery. They gathered and passed on knowledge of natural medicines; treatments like ragwort, garlic, echinacea, which these days, Mabel knows, are sold for high prices by big drug companies.

But their roles were always unpaid, unrecorded and almost entirely overlooked.

Men, on the other hand, did medicine in public. They got themselves trained (but banned women from universities until 150 years ago), practised in hospitals (closed to women until 100 years ago), and had their findings and opinions recorded and taken seriously. Because men also ran governments, businesses, the legal profession, armies, newspapers and almost all public institutions (women weren't even allowed to vote until 1920 in the US, and 1928 in England) men's medicine was the one people noticed.

Even so, Mabel is proud to notice, *lots* of women made it in the men's medical world. Women like adviser to the Pope, Hildegard von Bingen in 1170, who built infirmaries for the sick; the mystic Mechthild of Magdeburg who provided medicines to the poor in 1275. There was American Mary Putnam, the first scientist in the 1800s to work on brain tumors, and in the 1860s, Marie Curie and her daughter Irene, (both of whom won Nobel Prizes in Chemistry; Marie won twice!).

Not to mention the first woman doctor in the English-speaking world, Elizabeth Blackwell, who was banned from twenty-nine medical schools, because she was a girl, before finally graduating in 1849, only to find that no hospital would let her in. Never one to give up, she started her own, for women and children.

And what's this… Mabel blinks. Even when the women made it, sometimes the men claimed the ideas and the credit. Like one of the greatest discoveries of all time, the double helix (the shape of DNA, the stuff genes are made of). It was reputed to be 33-year-old Rosalind Franklin's techniques that first showed the structure in 1953, but her rival James Watson and his friend Francis Crick got the Nobel Prize for it in 1962. Some say she never got over it; she died of cancer at only thirty-seven.

Women had the picture all right; they just weren't allowed into it!

"MABEL!"

Mabel jumps a meter in the air! Her smart (but sneaky) mother is standing right behind her, staring at the screen. Heart thumping, Mabel looks back at it and… it's blank. Mum ruffles her hair, tells her firmly it's bed-time and leaves.

The screen throbs wickedly red and the shiny wet disk slips out. Mabel hides it and goes to bed.

"Aaah-aah-aah-tschoo!" Globs of snot splatter the screen. Mabel mops it and herself up. It's the next day and her cold is worse. Blowing her nose, she wonders crossly which genius will cure catchy germs like colds and flu and… the screen lights up… and it's a big strapping girl!

Oh yuck!

strike 5
go to
page 51

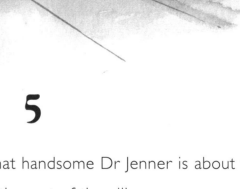

STRIKE 5

Sara Nelmes, milkmaid, is antsy with excitement. That handsome Dr Jenner is about to do an experiment which will either kill little James Phipps, or save the rest of the village.

Everyone is dying hideous deaths from the angry, red, pus-filled boils of smallpox, the horror plague that is killing 600,000 people every year, except the young women who milk cows and catch cowpox. Dr Jenner has noticed that cowpox has made Sara's milkmaid girlfriends safe from smallpox and now Sara's got the cowpox and he's going to test his theory out on Jimmy.

It's Saturday, May 14, 1796, Berkeley, England. Edward Jenner takes pus from Sara's cowpox boil and scratches it into 8-year-old Jimmy. Jimmy gets cowpox and seven weeks later he recovers. Then, the moment of truth, Jenner scratches deadly smallpox pus into Jimmy.

Mabel's heart is thumping.

And Jimmy remains as fit as a fiddle! The cowpox made him immune to smallpox! Vaccination (from the Latin word "vacca" for "cow") is born.

more on edward jenner go to page 52

strike 6 go to page 54

MORE ON EDWARD JENNER

What Jenner did would not be allowed today; risking someone's life to try out a new idea. Many people did in those days though, including Jenner's teacher, the brilliant Scot, John Hunter. In 1767, he injects himself with what he thinks is the disease gonorrhea, to prove it's different from syphilis; only it is syphilis, and he later dies of it.

In 3000 BC the Chinese stuffed powdered smallpox scabs (YUCK!) up the noses of children to make them immune to it (it worked) because they and lots of other people in other countries after them noticed that if someone gets smallpox and survives, they don't get it again.

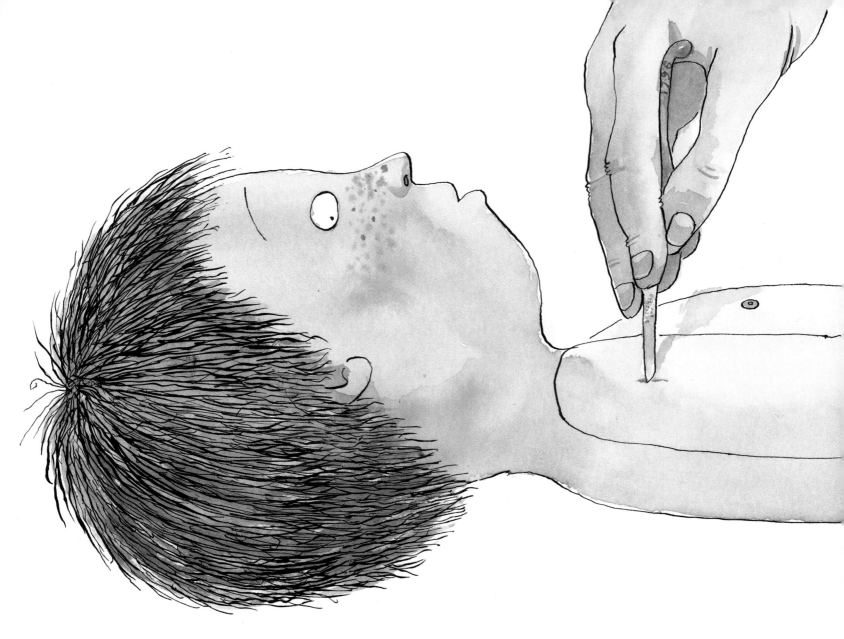

Jenner himself is rejected and sneered at by the medical establishment before vaccination catches on, but he remains humble and peaceful; writing poems, playing the flute and vaccinating the poor for free. When 8-year-old James Phipps grows up, Jenner builds him a cottage and plants roses in the garden himself.

Today, there is no smallpox. Vaccination had wiped it off the face of the earth by November 1974.

But there are still many more deadly epidemics…

An orchestra strikes up another tune…

STRIKE 6

The joker is dizzy with dancing, when suddenly his legs go cold. He rips off his mask, falls to the floor, his face violet-blue. This joker isn't joking! Everyone at the fancy dress ball panics, guests are rushed to hospital and die, buried in their gaudy costumes, the first victims of the Great Cholera epidemic of Paris, 1832.

Cholera spreads to London, killing thousands, and in 1854, turns John Snow (doctor to the poor) into a detective.

Everyone else thinks cholera is a poison being spread by evil strangers. While people panic, attack each other on the street, and hack each other to death, Snow investigates. He notices that although everyone around a particular street in London is getting cholera, the workers in the nearby brewery aren't. The only difference he can find is that the workers don't drink from the Broad Street water pump. John concludes that cholera is in the water.

(Mabel's not surprised. She looks at the filthy conditions. People defecate into rivers. There are open sewers in the street and ponds of feces and urine in backyards; all of it seeping through the earth into the underground wells of water that people pump up and drink!)

It turns out Snow is right; he is the first to discover that cholera is caused by the invisible living things that come from contaminated water.

Florence Nightingale, back from cleaning up the Crimean War, gets the government to "clean up", and water slowly becomes purer.

(Mabel notes sadly that 2000 years before, the Romans already had clean water provided by sewerage and aqueducts; not because they knew about germs, but because they noticed people were healthier in clean surroundings.)

strike 7 more plagues die go to page 56

And now a terrible deep growl.

STRIKE 7
MORE PLAGUES DIE

The mad dog leaps, its eyes glowing red, foam splattering from its mouth. Mabel cries out, and the little boy goes down, fighting uselessly as the dog's fangs tear into his flesh again and again.

The dog has rabies, and now 9-year-old Joseph Meiser will get it too – hideous pain, madness and a convulsing death.

It's July 1885, Paris, and Mrs Meiser knows that the brilliant scientist, Louis Pasteur, has been working on a vaccine for rabies. She begs him to try "the cure" on her boy, even if it's not ready. Pasteur tries it. It works.

Ah, but six years before, Mabel sees another lucky break...

It's 1879 and Louis Pasteur has just done something dumb! He's gone on holidays and forgotten the experiment he's in the middle of back home.

He'd been trying to prove that diseases are caused not by bad air or poisons, but by living invisible things; microbes. So he'd been growing the nasty cholera germ in a broth in his lab, to give to healthy chickens to show they will catch cholera from it. Only he left the broth on the bench.

When he gets home, it's stale; the cholera in it is weak, but he gives it to the chickens anyway. Disaster! They don't get sick.

Pasteur is intrigued. He brews up some fresh, new, cholera broth, gives it to the same chickens, as well as some new chickens. The new ones get cholera and die. The old ones (who got the stale broth first) stay well. The weak cholera in the stale broth has immunized the chickens!

Pasteur has invented a cholera vaccine by *chance*. (He didn't know it then, but the whole idea of vaccines is that you give someone a *weak* strain of a disease so they become immune to it, not sick; then when they meet the *deadly* strain, their body just shrugs it off.)

So Pasteur decides to try the same idea with a disease that's wiping out France's cows and sheep; anthrax. This time he deliberately brews up the anthrax germ, leaves it until it goes weak and then gives it to some sheep and cows. Some weeks later in a stunning photo opportunity in front of reporters and a crowd, he tests the vaccine by injecting the same animals with the deadly anthrax... and the animals don't get sick. Pasteur uses the same logic to make young Joe Meiser's vaccine - weakening the rabies virus so that it protects not kills. He uses a completely different approach to kill lots of other germs by heating them (germs in milk, beer, wine and silk worms, which have been souring, rotting and fermenting those products and bankrupting farmers). He saves those industries and what's more, pasteurized milk is born!

The cash value of his discoveries is reckoned to be as much as the cost charged by Germany for the 1870-71 war. He is voted more popular than Napoleon or Charlemagne, but his 12-year-old daughter still dies of typhoid fifteen years before that germ is found.

And these days, Mabel knows, there are vaccines to prevent measles, mumps, rubella, tetanus, diptheria, whooping cough, polio, yellow fever, hepatitis A and B, typhoid, meningococcal meningitis, Japanese encephalitis. A vast tide of humanity has been saved by vaccination, although only in those countries which can afford to give the injections.

another lucky break
go to page 58

ANOTHER LUCKY BREAK

A little man is humming…

It's 1928 and Alexander Fleming is on holiday, away from his divinely dirty lab, where he grows all sort of lovely germs in plates of jelly. (Although really he's trying to find out about the "staph" germ, which gets into people through cuts or through the mouth, and kills them in a huge number of truly inventive ways.)

But when he gets back to London, and starts tossing out the old plates, he sees that one has mold growing on it. That irritating chap on the floor above grows molds to study them; a spore must have floated down and in through Alex's window. He looks closer and sees the staph germs he'd been growing have disappeared in the area around the mold. The mold has made a liquid that has killed the germs! Alexander Fleming calls the liquid "penicillin" after the mold's name "penicillium", and the world has its first antibiotic. But not enough… Fleming can't get more than a speck of penicillin from his molds. Until…

more on alex go to page 59

MORE ON ALEX

This "lucky break" is not a bolt from the blue, Mabel notices.

In the 5th century BC, the ancient Greeks write of molds as therapies; in the 1800s, several French scientists, including Pasteur, note that bacteria won't grow in broth when mold gets to it.

Gooddess be! I dot add bold kill gerbs

In 1897 a French medical student even proves that penicillin stops bacteria growing in animals, but he dies young and without fame.

Alex Fleming is a very lucky man. Earlier, in 1921, he discovers another antibiotic by accident. He has a cold and sneezes on to one of his staph germ plates, and then notices that his snot has killed the germs. So he tests a whole bunch of runny, yucky things... and finds out that egg white and tears kill germs too. He has discovered lysozyme, a common antibiotic, but of limited use. He pays small children to cry, and squirts lemon juice into his visitors' eyes to get more tears.

Although he is not the first to understand the power of tears.

Thousands of years before, in Mesopotamia, sliced onions were put on sore eyes; the tears cured the problem.
But penicillin is to prove the big winner...

war on germs go to page 60

WAR ON GERMS

The whine of the bombs, the rush of the flame-throwers, the rumble of the tanks. Soldiers splattered and torn by the "modern" weapons of World War II. It's 1941, thirteen years after Alex's discovery, and if the weapons don't kill people, germs will. The pressure is on to get this "penicillin" to the thousands of soldiers who are dying from infected wounds.

But there's a problem. Only one two-millionth of the liquid made by Fleming's mold is penicillin! How to get enough?

Safely tucked away at Oxford University in England, Australian Howard Florey and co-worker, Ernst Chain, start feverishly working to stockpile penicillin. They grow the mold in milk churns, lemonade bottles, bedpans and a bathtub, and can't even get enough penicillin to treat one staph-infected cop. They know the Americans have the technology, so, with the bombs raining down on London, Florey crosses the submarine-infested Atlantic in desperation and begs for help.

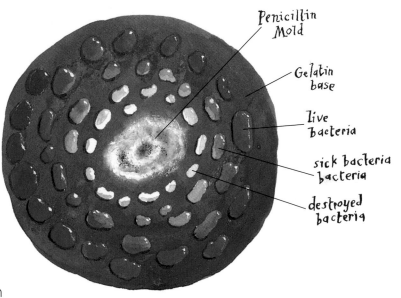

PENICILLIN
AT WORK

In exchange for the patent, the Americans work with Florey and brew up great vats of penicillin. Florey takes it to the soldiers in the field, and penicillin saves tens of thousands of lives. Chain, Florey and Fleming share the 1945 Nobel Prize.

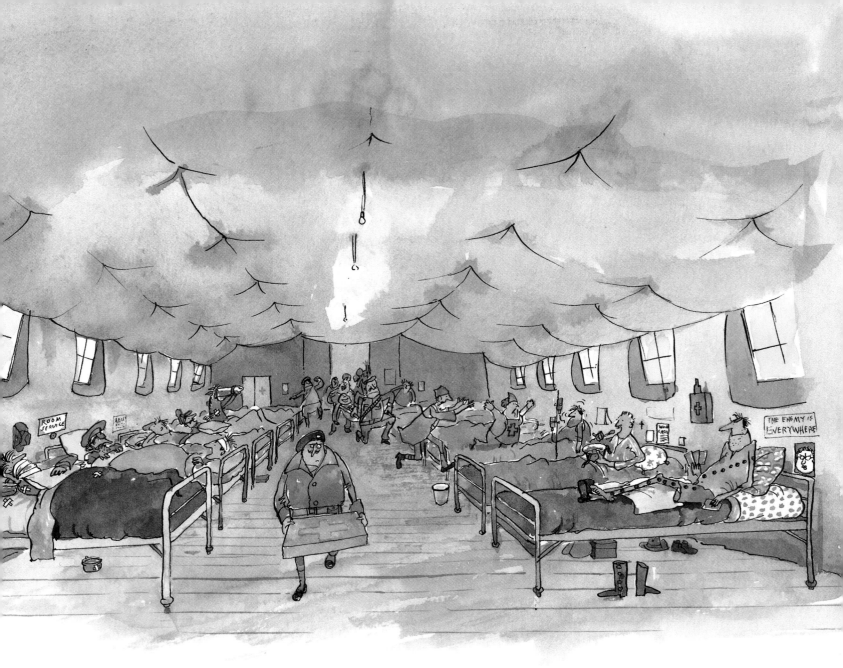

Mabel knows the rest! Her Grandpa tells her every Veterans' Day (Remembrance Day) about the miraculous arrival of penicillin in his tent-hospital in France during the war. It had saved the life of his best buddy, and, Grandpa says, it's only been recently (well, to him, but really in the last fifty or so years) that most of the medicines that Mabel takes for granted were invented. Medicines like all the other antibiotics, anti-malarials, anti-histamines, anti-coagulants, non-explosive anesthetics, the birth control pill, steroids, immunosuppressives, drugs against diabetes, gout, leukemia and some other cancers, Parkinson's, peptic ulcers, and drugs for mental illnesses.

Grandpa himself swears he was saved by that new-fangled blood transfusion.

Yeah, right Grandpa. Blood transfusions are a REAL miracle… NOT!

The screen hisses at her, and Mabel looks up, startled.

body wars
go to
page 62

BODY WARS

A sheep bleats and bleeds into the arm of a slightly crazy young divinity student called Arthur Coga. The gathered doctors hold their collective breath. 1667, and members of the Royal Society are gathered in London to watch Dr Richard Lower perform Britain's first blood transfusion. From time immemorial, people have believed that receiving blood from outside will cure ills, promote health and save lives. But it doesn't make Arthur sane.

Then – DISASTER! – a man DIES after getting a blood transfusion. Even though it turns out that the patient's wife poisoned him, blood transfusions get a bad name, and nothing much happens for 250 years.

From time to time, a doctor does try to transfuse blood from one person to another, and it's a mess; the blood coming out keeps clotting before it goes in to the next person. It's not until 1909 that the Austrian Dr Karl Landsteiner makes it work. He proves that blood comes in three varieties (A, B and O), and blood going in has to match the blood already there. Sir Almoth Wright (who is Alex Fleming's mentor and known as Sir Almost Right) works out how to stop blood clotting, so BINGO, blood can be stored. Soon it is taken, sorted, stored and matched, ready for both the 1st and 2nd World Wars, for soldiers like Mabel's 18-year-old Grandpa in 1944. Poor Landsteiner dies the year before, of a blood clot!

BLOOD TRANSFUSION

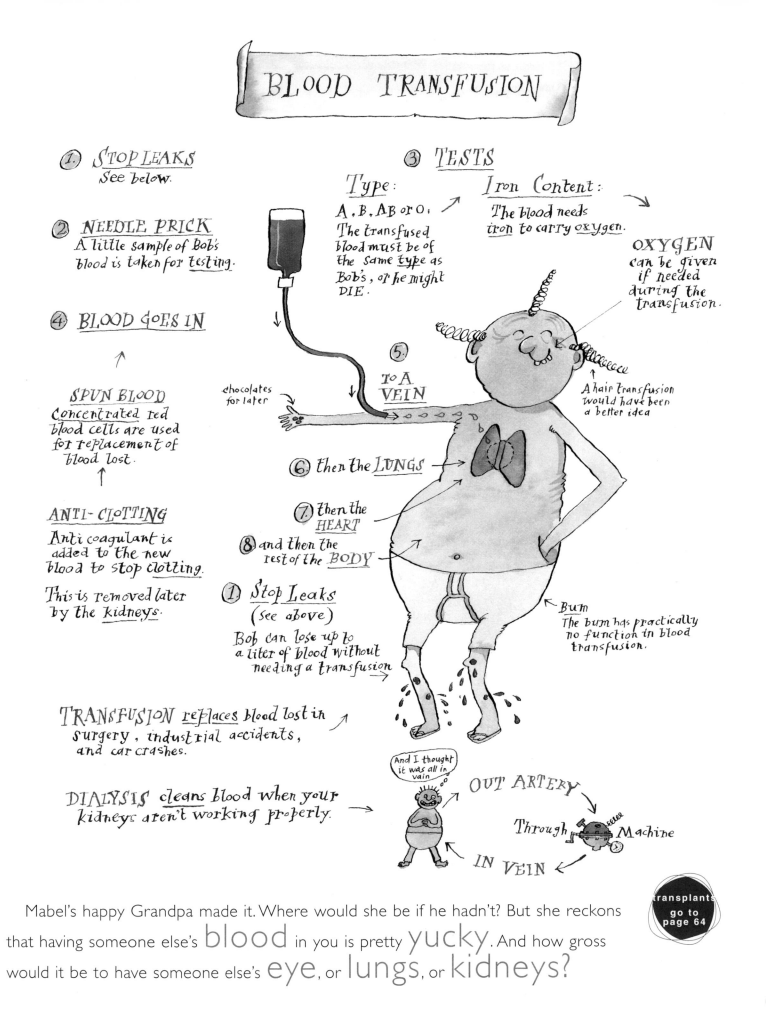

① **STOP LEAKS**
See below.

② **NEEDLE PRICK**
A little sample of Bob's blood is taken for testing.

③ **TESTS**

Type:
A, B, AB or O.
The transfused blood must be of the same type as Bob's, or he might DIE.

Iron Content:
The blood needs iron to carry oxygen.

OXYGEN can be given if needed during the transfusion.

④ **BLOOD GOES IN**

SPUN BLOOD Concentrated red blood cells are used for replacement of blood lost.

ANTI-CLOTTING
Anti coagulant is added to the new blood to stop clotting.

This is removed later by the kidneys.

⑤ TO A VEIN

A hair transfusion would have been a better idea

chocolates for later

⑥ then the **LUNGS**

⑦ then the **HEART**

⑧ and then the rest of the **BODY**

Bum
The bum has practically no function in blood transfusion.

① **Stop Leaks**
(See above)

Bob can lose up to a liter of blood without needing a transfusion

TRANSFUSION replaces blood lost in surgery, industrial accidents, and car crashes.

DIALYSIS cleans blood when your kidneys aren't working properly.

And I thought it was all in vain

OUT ARTERY

Through Machine

IN VEIN

Mabel's happy Grandpa made it. Where would she be if he hadn't? But she reckons that having someone else's blood in you is pretty yucky. And how gross would it be to have someone else's eye, or lungs, or kidneys?

transplants go to page 64

TRANSPLANTS

Wrrrr click wrrrr click. Mabel's zoomed back to 3,000 years ago.

In 800 BC, the Indians are doing a brisk trade in nose transplants. If men cheat on their wives, they get their noses cut off. So a leaf is used as a stencil on their cheek, the skin is cut around it then removed and whacked on the (empty) nose-place and two reeds shoved up for air. For real transplants, the nose of a slave is sewn on instead!

And, over a thousand years later, Mabel sees two befuddled brothers from Asia Minor, Cosmas and Damian, perform the miracle of the first leg transplant, (only they put a black leg on a white body!). They become Patron Saints of Medicine after being burnt, stoned, cut in half and finally beheaded for being unorthodox.

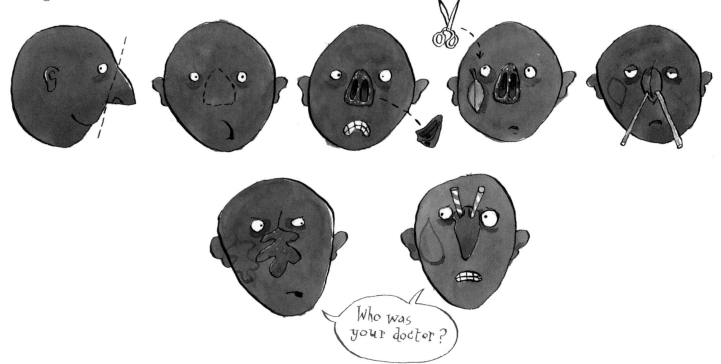

Who was your doctor?

Then nothing but nose transplants, body bits sewn on not put in the body, for 1500 years. They're not put in because it turns out that body parts are like blood; the ones going in have to match what's already there or the body fights them off. And this bamboozles scientists for thousands of years, until the 1950s, when the Australian, Macfarlane Burnet and his colleague, Medawar, work out why bodies attack a stranger's organ. Soon, drugs are made to dampen the fight, and by 1954, body parts start flying. Kidneys, lungs and livers of the newly-dead find homes in other people's bodies until the last bastion…

Oh, for heaven's sake...
'Gimme an 'H';
Gimme an 'E'
Gimme an A , R , T...'

Omigod...
Which is
Which?

Mabel sees Denise Darvall, just 24 years old, in a car in South Africa. The car crashes and Denise's brain dies. Her still-beating heart is taken from her.

In a move that shocks the world, 45-year-old Christiaan Barnard puts that heart into the waiting chest of 54-year-old Louis Washkansky. For eighteen days he lives, Denise's heart beating on in his chest. Beating on. And on… and on…

'Two-Left-Feet'
Syndrome

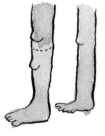

Look twice,
Cut once
rule

Cosmas – Damian
Syndrome

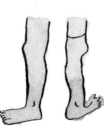

Circular Walk
Syndrome

SOME TRAPS for NOVICE SURGEONS

And on. and on. The heart throbs, filling the screen. The room vibrates, the thumping surrounds Mabel. Everything pulses red and suddenly she is flung back hard against her chair, as if taking off in a jet. The screen is running jagged and wild and it starts to wail; a thin, high chipmunk garble.

And now Mabel sees a sheep standing next to itself, its clone; a cow created from its own milk; twins born years apart; old women having babies; part-human pigs whose hearts are being placed inside sick people; and Mabel cries out.

But still the future rushes out at her. Infertile women give birth to themselves, dead children are cloned so parents can have them back, diseases are cured by sniffing in someone else's genes. Health, youth and beauty can be bought or engineered from a human gene bank; the rich re-design and copy themselves and their children, while the poor still die from diseases of the past. The pitch of human clamoring rises higher and higher until it's screeching inside Mabel's head.

She slams the disk eject.

And everything stops.

Mabel never finds the disk again. There is no record of her miracles anywhere but in her brain.

But then she picks up the paper some months later and sees,

Designer Transplants... a triumph for human cloning

Mabel reads that people with failing eyes or livers or kidneys or hearts will soon be able to clone themselves (by having their genes injected into a woman's egg, then put in her womb to grow as an embryo) and then kill this tiny copy of themselves and take the organs they need for transplantation, to replace their damaged parts. A perfect match! No rejection! No drugs!

Mabel wonders, would she do it?

Would she be like Horace and Paré, Pasteur, Nightingale and Barnard? Would she take the chance?

What is a miracle?

And what is a monstrosity?

Mabel, quite well now, takes Max and goes out to play.

INDEX

GAEL JENNINGS

Despite having spent more than a decade in a labcoat, Gael Jennings is actually really a glamorous TV personality with a PhD (in how the immune system works - but don't ask her how) and a few million awards for her TV stories on science and medicine (well a dozen). After eight years in medical research (looking for HIV, B cells and sperm), she turned from doing science to talking about it, working for the Australian Broadcasting Corporation for thirteen years - including science and medical reporting for TV news, "The 7.30 Report", "Quantum" and her own daily show on metropolitan radio, 3LO.

Now she's writing about it.

Gael's greatest joys are her three kids, her friends and finding things out. This is her first book.

ROLAND HARVEY

Roland Harvey has been illustrating since he was two. He is well-known for the idiosyncratic style which is reflected in all his books, including the popular *My Place in Space* (Honour Book, Children's Book Council of Australia) and *The Friends of Emily Culpepper* (commended by the Children's Book Council). *Burke and Wills*, part of Roland's unique Australian history series, was awarded the Clifton Pugh Award for illustration.

Roland's most recent books are *Islands in My Garden* by Jim Howes, winner of the 1999 Wilderness Society Award for Children's Literature, *The Six Wonders of Wobbly Bridge*, written by Gwenda Smyth, *What's a Bunyip?* by Nette Hilton and *Bass and Flinders* by Cathy Dodson. Roland now knows about space, insects, history and disease.

ACKNOWLEDGEMENTS

Undying (sorry!) gratitude to many people who guided, coaxed, and nursed us through various operations: Professor Michael Nott, Dr Richard Travers, Professor Graham Brown and Dr Michael Rozen, for expressing various degrees of horror and professional concern; Malcolm Forsyth and Sharon Sperling at the Australian Red Cross Blood Service; Carolyn Harrington; and designing women Carlie O'Brien and Petrina Griffin for pulling it all together superbly. Thanks to Vicki Zimitat for her enthusiastic internet research, and to Kate Ryan and Dinah Lewis for keeping me off the straight and narrow.

Gael wishes to thank Jenni Smith for the title *Sick As* (Australian edition) and for introducing the CD-ROM to Mabel.

[1] Letter to the Royal Society September 17, 1683 from University of California, Museum of Paleontology, Berkeley Website.